Project Management

Everything You Need to Start, Get Through and Finish Projects Successfully

Konrad Obidoski

Table of Contents

Konrad Obidoski

Introduction

I want to thank you and congratulate you for purchasing the book, *"Project Management: Everything You Need to Start, Get Through and Finish Projects Successfully"*.

This book will give you practical and well-tested strategies that will make project management easy, doable and fun. No longer will you be daunted by the term "project management" as you will be equipped with proper skills and information to handle any task that may be assigned to you.

If you are currently managing a project from scratch, use this book to guide you along the way. You can count on the fact that you will end up with positive results in your project.

Thanks again for purchasing this book, I hope you enjoy it!

Konrad Obidoski

Chapter 1

Planning a Project

Before you even start evaluating how you will proceed with your plan, you need to understand what Management is. Management is one of the most important aspect for the financial success of a business. It has been noted by many that without proper management, no business can make profits in the long run. Hence, before you even take up a project, you need to evaluate what management is, its importance and how to do it right.

Management is basically a huge process that requires a lot of work. The basic goal behind management is to make sure that you get things done in time. That is all management is concerned about, to make sure that the business achieves its required goals in times without any hurdles or problems. In this process, the business has to make sure that it is being efficient as well effective. So, let's jump into how a business can be effective and efficient.

Effectiveness & Efficiency

Effectiveness basically means completing the task. Whatever goal is assigned to a person, he has to make sure that he completes it within the stipulated time. Effectiveness simply means that you provide an end result. Efficiency on the other hand means doing the things correctly. Yes, the end result is very important but at the same time being efficient along the way is important to, you can't just use as many resources as you want or spend thousands of dollars on a small task. There is an order to everything. Efficiency can always be increased by many ways, such as

> ➤ Making sure that you use fewer inputs in the process of production. If you are using too many inputs and wasting your money on them, then you can never be efficient. You might be able to complete a task but at what cost, you'll have achieved an end result but along the way you wasted so much money that the firm can't make any profits now. Hence, make sure that the amount of inputs that you use in the business is ideal depending on the size of the organization.

➢ Another way to be efficient is to make sure that the amount of output that you are generating is the same but still the amount of cost incurred on the inputs is less, basically you are using fewer resources to produce the same amount. This way you are working better and saving costs. This will definitely help in increasing the profits

Hence, for a business to be successful it has to be effective as well as efficient. Every business out there wants to make sure that their profits are the highest, so they are mostly concerned about efficiency only. Therefore, they sacrifice on effectiveness. The end result that they achieve by doing this leads to lack of customer satisfaction. The products might not be up to the mark because of cost cutting. If a business wants to be successful then it has to be effective and efficient. These two terms need to always work together and are correlated. A business has to make sure that it is achieving the required goals, that is, it is being effective and at the same doing it in such a way that it leads to the highest profits, that is, it being effective.

A great example here to help you better understand the two concepts is that, say in a firm a boss gives his junior a task to produce 200 unites of a good, the person does achieve the task and very easily too but at the same time he did this work by operating on double shift. He also wasted resources because a batch turned out to be faulty. Hence, the person was effective because he achieved the goal but not efficient because he couldn't minimize the costs rather he increased them. Say, he does work efficiently and reduces cost substantially but he isn't able to make the required products. Instead of producing two hundred units he only produces one fifty units. This way he wasn't efficient. The best way to achieve the goal would have been to complete the required task of producing two hundred units and at the time minimizing the cost as far as possible.

Management Process

Management is a huge process, it requires you to complete a lot of tasks and it is a lot of work. But in the end management is worth it because it helps you to complete the task on time and with increased profits. The management process is basically all the things that managers are required to do in order to achieve the goals. Managers have to contemplate who will perform which task and in what way. This way they can increase the efficiency and also be effective. The basic purpose of this is to not make up plans as we go but to rather work on it now, so that we are ready for any mishaps that may happen in the future. The process of management has five major tasks, they are as follow:

1. **Planning** – It is the most important function of management; it basically determines what the business will do. The managers sit around and go over all the conditions that are prevailing in the market and on that basis they decide what the business will do. They plan in advance what the goal of the firm would be and how the firm will achieve the said goals.

2. **Organizing** – It is the second step in the process of management; it basically requires managers to organize the whole business, to tell people what they will do by giving them duties, assigning tasks to everyone so they know what they have to do and also grouping people together that can work together as a team. It also requires the managers to set up bosses over everyone, so that there is somebody there to control what goes on in the firm. This way the subordinates have to report their progress to the assigned superior and the managers can judge the performance of the organization. The managers also make up plans regarding the amount of resources that will be used and in what way. This is to ensure that no resources are wasted and efficiency is maintained in the organization.

3. **Staffing** – It is the third step in the process of management. Staffing is the most important function of management because unless and until you have the required personnel, you won't ever be able to complete a task. Staffing basically means hiring people depending upon the needs of the organization as well as the qualifications of the perspective employee. You have to find the right person to do the right job because otherwise they will definitely not be able to complete the task assigned to them on time. There are various activities that are included inside staffing such as selection, placement, training and development and recruitment. It is basically the job of the human resource department to deal with the hiring of personnel; this is why staffing is also known as the human resource process of management.

4. **Directing** – It means that the person who is in charge tells the subordinates what exactly they have to do. It also means that he makes sure that they do it in a correct way. Directing does not just end when you assign a task to someone, to make sure that they actually complete the task, you have to stay on their head at all times. You have to get reports from them to check that they are working correctly and at the same time are able to achieve their deadlines. There are a lot of aspects that are within

directing. Directing is the most difficult process of management because you have to ensure that the person giving the orders can actually see the task through without any problems.

The various aspects that are part of directing are leading people to set an example that they can follow, influencing them to give their best, this way the amount of work that they are able to do in just a few hours will increase. It also involves motivating the employees because sometimes the employees are not motivated enough to actually work, this delays the task as they are not able to work due to lack of interest. Hence, the manager has to make sure that he motivates them to give their best. He has to build a nice atmosphere of trust where the employee feels secure enough to share his problems so that the superior can help him work through them. This will help the employee to be more efficient as well as effective. The two major parts of directing are motivation and leadership; both of them have to go hand in hand if a person wants to successfully achieve a task. Motivation basically means to give the employees enough incentives by updating their environment with positivity that they feel like working even more. Leadership on the other hand is basically telling people what they have to do by setting an example; you have to influence people to give their best. This way the workers do the work willingly and also happily. A person has to be a good communicator if he wants to be good at directing. He should be able to get his message across to his subordinates and should have the power in his voice that everyone listens to him otherwise nobody would take him seriously. A director has to be nice and supple enough to influence people but at the same time he needs to be harsh and strong to take the required decisions.

5. **Controlling** – It is the last process in the management function. It is basically required to help measure how the firm is doing. The firm has to calculate data from various sources and then decide how well it is doing; hence, the firm measures its own performance. The performance is measured on the basis of the goals of the organization that were achieved during the year. These goals are the same goals that were set up during planning, which is the first process of management. Controlling is done through various ways but mostly, the first step is to setup certain standards, these standards are nothing more than what the firm actually wishes to achieve. The manger decides what the performance of the firm should be and that becomes the standard against which the performance is compared. Then, the firm has to go around checking what

its actual performance is. This is mostly done in terms of the profits received or the sales made. Then of course the next step is to compare the actual performance with the standards that were made. This tells us if there are any disparities in terms of reaching the goals of the organization. Hence, the firm knows how far behind or ahead it is in the performance that it wanted to achieve, so it can take the necessary steps to correct these problems. In the end the firm has to take certain actions to ensure that its goals are achieved.

What does Management consist of?

The best way to understand what management really is, is to make sure that you know what it actually consists of. If you understand what management really is and what is its role in the organization then you can better hire managers that suit your need. Hence, you need to know what the nature of management is and why people say that it is important.

1. **Management is concerned only with the end result**: The major purpose of management is to ensure that the goals of the organization are achieved on times. This is the first step in the process of management. The managers' plan what the goals should be and the managers make sure that the firm achieves these set goals. They have

to closely monitor the situation of the firm to ensure that there are no deviations in terms of the actual performance. Hence, management ensures that the firm is always on the right path.

Every firm has a few goals that they really want to achieve at the end of the year, such as, to increase their sales, to maximize their profits, to develop more goodwill, to get return on investment by 10%. Management makes sure that the whole firm works together. It ensures that nobody in the firm is working in the wrong direction and hence, the organization goals are achieved on time. If there was no management then it would have been very difficult to coordinate the efforts of the different branches of the organization and it may have been very difficult to actually achieve their goals. Management ensures that everyone is working together in the right direction.

2. **Management is all about teamwork**: Management makes sure that everyone works together. There are numerous people that work in organization and each with his/her own diverse needs. These people may even be from different cultures and from different countries, in such a situation it can be very difficult to make sure that the communication within the organization is sound enough

and everyone is able to work with each other without any problems. Management instills team spirit within the organization; this makes sure that everyone works together to achieve the goals of the firm instead of working in different directions, which never leads to any good. Management helps the whole organization to focus upon the major goals of achieving the set standards instead of being concerned about their own wellbeing. Management coordinates work between different departments or branches so that the whole organization can work together in a better way. This is the basic purpose of management. To makes sure that the whole organization is organized and hence, can work more effectively and efficiently.

3. **Management cannot be touched**: It is very obvious that management is actually intangible. You will never be able to see where management is or is it even actually functioning but in end its presence can be felt in terms of better performance of the organization. The presence can also be felt when the whole organization works hard enough to achieve the required goals, when the employees are getting the correct salary and hence there is no disquiet within the firm, when the working environment is positive or when there is order in terms of the functioning of the firm, etc.

4. **Management is present at all levels**: Management is required and is present in all organizations. It isn't just your organization that requires management but every organization in the world. There is no organization in the world in which such activities that are concerned with management are not carried out. All the organizations even if they are the top five hundred companies of the world or the smallest of the firms or even a local business require some sort of management. The difference is that huge firms have a lot of managers that are highly trained personnel who have a lot of experience in terms of managing organizations. The small firms may even have a few managers who might not be that highly trained but are still able to handle the management of the organization because of its small size. The proprietor might himself be the manager as well, as is the case in many small organizations. Hence, management in some form or the other is required at all levels.

Management isn't just required in organizations. It is so important that even schools or hospitals require management in one way or another. Without management the whole thing would fall apart, there might be chaos in many organizations if there is no management to control the work of the organization.

5. **Management in concerned with all of the activities of the firm**:   Management is multi-dimensional; it requires a lot of people to work together all of which may have diverse needs. Hence, management is a very unpredictable action, we don't when something might happen and hence the managers have to take the decisions accordingly. Management has three fundamental aspects that it focuses on:

- (a) Work Management: All firms exist for the execution of some work. In a plant, an item is made, in a clothing store a client's need is fulfilled regarding buying great clothes and in a hospital, a patient is dealt with. Management deciphers this work into small jobs that are to be accomplished by the respective employees and allocates resources so that there is a way to accomplish it. This is done in terms of issues to be explained, choices to be made, and arrangements to be set up, spending plans to be arranged, obligations to be allotted and power to be assigned.

- (b) Individual Management: Humans resources or individuals are an association's most noteworthy resources. In spite of all improvements in technology through innovation, completing the work through individuals is still a noteworthy errand for the supervisor. Overseeing individuals has two dimensions:

- (i) Managing representatives as people with differing needs and conduct;

  (ii) it likewise means managing people as a gathering of individuals.

- The objective of Management is to make sure individuals work towards the organization goals, so as to accomplish the association's objectives, to make sure that the qualities of each individual viable and their shortcomings unimportant.

- (c) Operations Management: Regardless of what the association, it has become an essential item for Management to keep in mind that the goal is to survive. This obliges a push action process that involves the stream of information material and the innovation for transforming this data into the required goals for utilization in the company's success. This is interlinked with both Work Management and Individual Management.

6. **Management is a nonstop process**: The procedure of management is a progression of ceaseless processes that keep on going; however it has separate capacities (Planning, Organizing, Directing, Staffing and Controlling). These processes are at the same time performed, constantly.

7. **Management is a team movement:** An association is an accumulation of assorted people with diverse needs. Each individual has an alternate reason for joining the association yet as individuals from the association they work towards satisfying the normal hierarchical objective. This obliges cooperation and coordination among the individual. In the meantime management ought to empower every one of its individuals to develop them and take care of their necessities as opportunities change.

8. **Management is an ever-changing function**: Management is a dynamic process and needs to adjust to the evolving environment. An association interfaces with its outer environment, which comprises of different social, monetary and political elements. Keeping in mind the end goal to be fruitful, an association must change itself and its objectives as per the earth's needs.

Konrad Obidoski

Chapter 2

Management Objectives

If you are starting a project there you have to make sure that you have certain objectives to achieve because otherwise it is almost impossible to get the required result. Hence, you have to makes sure that you understand the objectives that management has to achieve and include them in your project.

Management tries to accomplish certain objectives, which are the wanted desires of any organization. They are the fundamental reason for doing the business. Without setting up objectives, an organization has no goals that or ideas in terms of what it has to do. In any association there are diverse goals and Management needs to accomplish all objectives in a compelling and effective way. Objectives can be grouped into authoritative goals, social goals and individual goals.

i.   Hierarchical   Objectives/   Authoritative   Goals: Management is in charge of setting and accomplishing targets for the association. It needs to accomplish an assortment of targets in all territories considering the interest of all partners including, shareholders, workers, clients and the Management. The fundamental target of any association ought to be to use human and material assets to the maximum capacity without wasting any resources, i.e., to satisfy the monetary goals of a business. The monetary goals are survival, profit and development.

Survival: The essential goal of any business is survival. Management must endeavor to guarantee the association's survival. To survive, an association must acquire enough incomes to take care of expenses.

Profit: Negligible profits are insufficient for business. Management needs to guarantee that the association makes a benefit from its actions. Profit gives a fundamental motivator to the managers and that leads effective operation of the venture. Benefits are vital for taking care of expenses and dangers of the business.

Development: A business needs to add to its prospects over the long haul, for this it is vital for the business to develop. To stay in the business, Management must endeavor to completely increase the development capability of the association. Development of a business can be measured as far as increment in the quantity of workers, the quantity of items sold or the increment in capital venture, and so forth. There can be different pointers of development.

ii.   Social goals: It includes creating advantages for society through the workings of the organization. As a piece of society, each association whether it is business or non-business has a social commitment to satisfy. This alludes to reliably making money for different constituents of society. This incorporates utilizing natural well disposed systems for creation, giving vocation chances to the burdened segments of society and giving essential comforts like schools and crèches to workers.

iii.   Individual goals: Organizations are comprised of individuals who have distinctive identities, foundations, encounters and goals. They all want that their respective needs be met. They want to have an increased salary and they also do not want to work too hard, they want to make sure that they have respect in the society and over time develop as they work in the organization.

iv.   Significance of Management

Management is very important and has a lot of significance. You have to make sure that you understand the important of management before you indulge in starting a project. When you understand it's important, you will yourself try to work on effective and efficient management for your project.

i.   Management helps in accomplishing team objectives: Management is needed not to satisfy individual goals but rather to achieve the association's objectives. The job of a leader is to give a typical job to the each individual so that they can all contribute in accomplishing the general objective of the association.

ii.   Management builds effectiveness: The point of an administrator is to lessen expenses and expand profitability through better planning, organizing, directing, staffing and controlling the association's exercises.

iii.   Management makes a dynamic association: All associations are in such a business environment, that it is always showing signs of change. It is for the most part seen that people in an association oppose change as it frequently means moving from a recognizable, secure environment into a more up to date and all the more difficult one. Management assists individuals with adjusting to these progressions so that the association can work in the same way without any problems.

iv. Management helps in accomplishing individual destinations: A manager persuades and leads his group in such a way, to the point that each individual has the capacity to accomplish individual objectives while adding to the general hierarchical target. Through inspiration and initiative the Management helps people to create interest, participation and responsibility towards team achievement.

v. Management helps in the advancement of society: An organization has various objectives to fill the needs of the distinctive social culture that constitutes it. During the time spent satisfying all these, Management helps in the association's advancement and through that it helps in the improvement of society. It serves to give great quality items and increases livelihood opportunities, embraces new technology for more prominent benefits of the general population and leads the way towards development and advancement.

Konrad Obidoski

Chapter 3

Levels of Management

If you have finally understood the important of management then you need to know the levels of management. There aren't only a few people that sit in a room that do management but rather a lot of them are divided into separate branches, each of which performs a very different function, hence, you have to make sure that you understand how the authority of the project should flow and what level performs what activity.

Top Management: It comprises of the senior most officials of the association by whatever name they are called. They are generally alluded to as the director, the CEO, boss working officer, president and Vice president. Top Management is a group comprising of chiefs from distinctive practical levels. Their essential undertaking is to incorporate assorted components and giving direction the exercises of distinctive offices as per the general targets of the association. These top-level supervisors are in charge of the welfare and survival of the association. They investigate the business environment and its suggestions for the association's survival. They figure general authoritative objectives and procedures for their accomplishment. They are in charge of the considerable number of exercises of the business and for its effect on society. The top level's work is mind boggling and unpleasant, requiring extended periods of time and responsibility to the association.

Center Management: It is the connection in the middle of top and lower level management. They are subordinate to top directors and better than the first line supervisors. They are normally known as divisional heads, operations administrator or plant director. Center Management is in charge of actualizing and controlling arrangements and methodologies created by top administration. In the meantime they are in charge of the considerable number of exercises of first line chiefs. Their primary errand is to do the arrangements defined by the top supervisors. For this they have to:

- Decipher the arrangements confined by top administration,

- Ensure that their area of expertise has the essential work force,

- Appoint essential obligations and duties to them,

- Rouse them to accomplish required goals,

- Co-work with different divisions for smooth working of the association. In the meantime they are in charge of the considerable number of exercises of first line chiefs.

Supervisory or Operational Administration: Foremen and lower level supervisors contain the lower level in the chain of command of the association. Administrators specifically supervise the workforce's endeavors. Their power and obligation is restricted by arrangements drawn by the top administration. Supervisory administration assumes a vital part in the association since they communicate with the real work force and go on directing based on the rules set by the center administration. Through their endeavors nature of yield is kept up, wastage of materials is minimized and security gauges are kept up. The nature of workmanship and the amount of yield relies on upon the diligent work, control and devotion of the specialists.

Elements of Management

Management has a lot of elements and each of them is as important as the next. If you want your project to be more successful then you have to understand these elements and work on them. These are not just things that management consists of but rather things that are required. Management is a long process that has been divided into many sub divisions. Each level creates such elements that the whole organization works together in achieving the goals.

Administration is portrayed as the procedure of arranging, sorting out, coordinating and controlling the endeavors of authoritative individuals and of utilizing hierarchical assets to accomplish particular objectives.

Planning is the capacity of deciding ahead of time what could possibly be done and who is to do it. This infers setting objectives ahead of time and building up a method for accomplishing them proficiently and viably. Planning can't forestall issues; however it can foresee them and get ready for emergency courses of action to manage them if and when they happen.

Organizing is the administration capacity of doling out obligations, gathering assignments, setting up power and designating of assets needed to do a particular arrangement. When a particular arrangement has been set up for the achievement of a hierarchical objective, the organizational objectives looks at the exercises and assets needed to actualize the arrangement. It figures out what exercises and assets are needed. It chooses who will do a specific undertaking, where it will be done, and when it will be finished. It includes the gathering of the obliged undertakings into sensible divisions or work units and the foundation of power and reporting connections inside of the hierarchical chain of importance. Legitimate hierarchical methods help in the achievement of work and advance both the proficiency of operations and the viability of results. Various types of business oblige diverse structures as indicated by the way of work.

Staffing is discovering the right individuals for the right occupation. An essential part of administration is to verify that the right individuals with the right capabilities are accessible at the right places and times to perform the association's objectives. This is otherwise called the human asset capacity and it includes exercises, for example, enrollment, choice, position and preparing of work force.

Directing includes driving, impacting and propelling representatives to perform the errands doled out to them. This obliges building up an environment that urges workers to put forth a valiant effort. Inspiration and administration are two key parts of course. Inspiring specialists implies essentially making a domain that makes them need to work. Authority is affecting others to do what you need them to do. A decent administrator coordinates through commendation and feedback in a manner that it draws out the best in the worker.

Controlling is the administration capacity of checking authoritative execution towards the achievement of hierarchical objectives. The assignment of controlling includes setting up norms of execution, measuring current execution, contrasting this and set up standards and making remedial move where any deviation is found. Here administration must figure out what exercises and yields are important for achievement, how and where they can be measured and who ought to have the power to make restorative move.

All of these processes together yield to the most important aspect of management, coordination.

Coordination — The Most Important Aspect of Management

If you really want your project to be successful then you have to ensure that there is coordination in your organization. This is because unless and until the whole organization will work together towards the achievement of certain goals, it is almost impossible to complete any task. Hence, you have to ensure that through management the whole organization would work together towards a single goal.

You have comprehended at this point that a manager needs to perform five interrelated activities during the time spent dealing with an association which is a framework made up of distinctive interlinked and reliant subsystems. A supervisor needs to interface these differing individuals towards the accomplishment of a typical objective. The procedure by which an administrator synchronizes the exercises of distinctive offices is known as coordination.

Coordination is the power that ties the various elements of Management. Coordination is here and there considered a different capacity of Management. It is the quintessence of Management, for accomplishing agreement among individual's endeavors and towards the achievement of organization objectives. Each administrative capacity is an activity contributing independently to coordination. Coordination is understood and intrinsic in all elements of an association. The procedure of planning the exercises of an association starts at the planning stage itself. Top Management makes goals for the whole association. The authoritative structure is then produced and staffed. Keeping in mind the end goal to guarantee that these arrangements are executed by coordination is needed. Any disparities in the middle of real and set up goals are then dealt with at the phase of controlling. It is through the procedure of coordination that a manager guarantees the organized course of action of individual and team endeavors. Coordination along these lines includes synchronization of the diverse activities or endeavors of the whole organization.

Coordination is ensuring that the organization works together so as to adjust to the different needs of individuals and keeping together the group spirit which is suitable for allotment of undertakings to the different individuals and seeing that the assignments are performed with agreement among the individuals themselves.

Nature of Coordination

(i) Coordination incorporates group endeavors: Coordination binds together irrelevant or assorted hobbies into deliberate work action. It gives a typical center to team work to guarantee that execution is as it was arranged and decided.

(ii) Coordination guarantees solidarity of activity: The reason for coordination is to secure solidarity of activity in the acknowledgment of a typical goal. It goes about as the coupling power in the middle of offices and guarantees that all activity is carried out for accomplishing the association's objectives.

(iii) Coordination is a nonstop process: Coordination is not a onetime work but rather a ceaseless procedure. It starts at the first stage and proceeds till controlling.

(iv) Coordination is an all-pervasive function: Coordination is needed at all levels of Management because of the discord in the way of working of different divisions. It coordinates the endeavors of distinctive divisions and diverse levels.

The sales, production and marketing department's endeavors must be facilitated for accomplishing authoritative objectives and goals concordantly. The purchase division is in charge of getting the goods. This then turns into the creation of products to be sold later on and lastly sales can occur.

(v) Coordination is the responsibility of all directors: Coordination is the capacity of each administrator in the association. Top-level managers need to facilitate with their subordinates to guarantee that the general strategies for the association are properly done. Center level Management organizes with both the top level and first line directors. Operational level Management works to ensure that the products are up to the marks and the quality is not diminished.

(vi) Coordination is a planned programme: An administrator needs to arrange the endeavors of distinctive individuals in a cognizant and intentional way. Indeed, even where individuals from a division energetically collaborate and work, coordination gives a course to that ready soul. Participation without coordination may prompt squandered exertion and coordination without collaboration may prompt disappointment among representatives.

Coordination, hence, is not a different capacity of Management, but rather it's extremely embodiment. For an association to viably and proficiently accomplish its destinations coordination is needed.

Chapter 4

Modern Management

The world is ever changing and if you want to complete any business project you have to learn to work based on the assumption that the world is connected. This is because if a manager wants to be successful in conducting a business project then he/she has to work on a worldwide level. Your project may not just effect your country or but rather the whole world, this institutes a need for worldwide management. Where a manager has to coordinate the efforts of many branches of a firm in different countries, also managing the firms that have been outsourced as well all the investors, shareholders, etc. that are from different cultural backgrounds. Hence, before beginning your project you have to understand why modern management is important and what are the basic things required from a modern manager.

Indeed, even as you read this part, the firms and their management are evolving. As society progresses, more and more technology is developed every day and countries get more connected, new technological innovation makes it conceivable to think about the world as a 'worldwide town', the extent of universal and intercultural connections is quickly extending. The current association is a worldwide association that must be overseen in a worldwide point of view. Hence, management is changing every day and for anyone to be more successful in this wake of life you have to adapt to these changes. Techniques of management have to be changed and even the way that we look at management. Firms have to find newer ways to conduct management that even involves the use of robots. The world is ever changing and if anyone wishes to be successful in management they have to adapt to these changes as quickly as possible.

Global Manager and the Difficulties that they face

Following the new international way of management, the worldwide manager needs to manage building up his organization's legitimate and business vicinity as a neighborhood office or business accomplice, reaching and arranging with customers, with lawful bodies including legal advisors and movement powers following the management changes including having specialized staff from different countries to be situated in another country that is different from their environment and culture, as likewise with nearby organizations offering enlistment managements. Another key part managers play is building up a proper database of the customers as to find potential customers for the beneficial outcomes of diverse and multi-social types of business activities that have now opened their doors on an international level such as outsourcing and worldwide conveyance, the manager has to also coordinate the efforts of such external business organizations.

The worldwide manager needs to guarantee that he finds himself able to source the right specialized abilities, fabricate an in number of asset based workings that are based on aptitudes, and have the capacity to convey on programming tasks to all the workers who are working for the organization in a globalized workplace.

There are various difficulties that a manager faces and he has to deal with all of them at the same time, these problems are very diverse and require special tactics. These are not just coordinating between offices on different continents but go as far as coordinating numerous time-zones, comprehension of customer's needs in light of the business timings that the customer's business works in, understanding and adjusting to the procedures and strategies that the customer is acquainted with. At last this capacity likewise incorporates clients desire for management, where the practical administrator needs to organize exercises in different countries as indicated by the client's needs, convey what is conceivable and what is unrealistic, and in like manner additionally deal with the desires and fulfillment levels of his own organization, the level of stress can be drastic and many organizations fail at such kind of things because they can't find the perfect manager to do the job for them.

The worldwide supervisor must be alive to changing business circumstances and client needs, he/she needs to stay informed regarding the patterns in outsourcing and has to evaluate any threats the business might face or anything that might lead to fall in the value of the business and also potential dangers. For instance, if a worldwide manager keeps on using the same outsourcing firm because it originates from their own country then that can be considered as discriminatory in nature because instead of using services that might be rendered at a cheaper price, the firm is rather trying to use services that help them in no way. If the firm takes the service of outsourcing from another country then they will have many benefits. Most African countries offer cheaper princes of production and also the government would then look favorably towards that organization which brought so much business for their country.

To condense, a worldwide supervisor today is one who has what can be termed as "multi -dimensional" sorts of abilities and additionally "gentler" sorts of aptitudes. Managers who comprehend investigation, procedure, designing, and innovation are as yet going to be required, yet amazingly the basic worldwide need is individuals who see how groups work and hence can influence them, understand how associations work and how individuals are motivated.

A supervisor who truly comprehends diverse societies ought to have the capacity to work in a western nation so that they can gain enough experience, then move on to work in the developing countries so that they can help their organization to build their empire and then finally work up the ladder back in perhaps the main office of the firm and be very quickly gainful in each of the three spots. It can in this manner be comprehended that the part of a worldwide administrator has developed similarly that the worldwide business and economy have advanced. It has changed from being a solitary dimensional part in a characterized business setting, to being a multi-faceted part that requires an assorted blend of specialized aptitudes, delicate management and relationship building abilities, and the capacity to soak up and learn new things.

Konrad Obidoski

Chapter 5

Planning

If you have finally understood what management is and how important it is. Then it is time to move on to the most important part of any project, which is planning. Planning is very important because without planning you cannot hope to achieve anything at all. Management teaches us that we need have order in the organization but unless and until we start planning how can we determine what it is to be done and who is to do it. Hence, Planning is the basis on which everything in a business organization is done. You have to make sure that you plan well because only then can you think of being successful

Planning is choosing ahead of time what to and how to do. It is one of the fundamental administrative capacities. Before doing something, the manager must plan how he will go about doing a particular task and achieving the required organization goals. Subsequently, Planning is firmly associated with inventiveness and advancement. Be that as it may, the manager would first need to set targets; at exactly that point will an administrator know where he needs to go. Planning tries to cross over any barrier between where we are and where we need to go. Planning is the thing that supervisors at all levels do. It obliges taking choices since it includes settling on a decision from various alternative courses of actions. Planning, accordingly, includes setting goals and creating proper strategies to accomplish these destinations. Targets give guidance to the organization. Without targets the organization would have no ideas how to perform different activities and what to do. If the firm has targets to achieve then it can work on them by assigning tasks and deciding what and how to produce. Otherwise, there will be chaos and no one will know how and what to do. Targets are important for every single administrative choice and activity. Planning gives a reasonable way to deal with accomplishing foreordained targets. All individuals, thus, need to work towards accomplishing hierarchical objectives. These objectives set the goals which should be accomplished and against which genuine execution is measured.

Accordingly, Planning means setting destinations and targets and a path to accomplish them. It is confusing what the targets are and what path will be taken by the organization, what could possibly be done how it is to be finished. The arrangement that is created needs to have a given time period however time is a restricted asset. It should be used reasonably. On the off chance that time component is not mulled over, conditions in the society may change and all strategies for success may go waste. Planning will be a pointless activity in the event that it is not followed up on or actualized.

Significance of Planning

Planning is surely critical as it lets us know where to go; it gives guidance and diminishes the danger of instability by planning conjectures. The significant advantages of Planning are:

(i) Planning gives a way: By expressing ahead of time how a function is to be done, Planning gives course to activity. Planning guarantees that the objectives or destinations are plainly expressed with the goal that they go about as an aide for choosing what move ought to be made and in which heading. On the off chance that objectives are very much characterized, workers are mindful of what the association needs to do and what they must do to accomplish those objectives. Offices and people in the association get to work in coordination. In the event that there was no Planning, representatives would be working in diverse bearings and the association would not have the capacity to accomplish its sought objectives.

(ii) Planning decreases the dangers of instability: Planning is an action that empowers a manager to look ahead and suspect changes. By choosing ahead of time the undertakings to be performed, Planning demonstrates the best approach to manage changes and indeterminate occasions. Changes or occasions can't be disposed of yet they can be expected and administrative reactions to them can be created.

(iii) Planning decreases inefficient exercises: Planning serves as the premise of organizing the exercises and endeavors of diverse divisions, offices and people. It helps in evading perplexity and misconception. Since, Planning guarantees clarity in thought and activity, work is carried on easily without interferences. Pointless and repetitive exercises are minimized or dispensed with. It is simpler to identify inefficiencies and take remedial measures to manage them.

(iv) Planning advances inventive thoughts: Since Planning is the first capacity of administration; new thoughts can take the state of solid arrangements. It is the most difficult action for the administration as it aids every single future activity prompting development and flourishing of the business. Hence, Planning requires that the managers come up with new and innovative plans so that the organization can work smoothly and have a competitive edge over its rivals.

(v) Planning encourages choice making: Planning helps the supervisors to investigate the future and settle on a decision from amongst different game plans. The chief needs to assess every option and select the most reasonable recommendation. Planning includes setting targets and anticipating future conditions, and helping in taking judicious choices.

(vi) Planning sets up gauges for controlling: Planning includes setting of objectives. The whole administrative procedure is worried with finishing foreordained objectives through Planning, sorting out, staffing, coordinating and controlling. Planning gives the benchmarks against which genuine execution is measured. By contrasting genuine execution and some standard, managers can know whether they have really possessed the capacity to accomplish the objectives. On the off chance that there is any deviation it can be adjusted. Along these lines, we can say that Planning is essential for controlling. On the off chance that there were no objectives and measures, then discovering deviations which are a part of controlling would not be conceivable. Hence, Planning gives the premise of control.

Components of Planning

(i) Planning spotlights on accomplishing targets: Organizations are set up with a broad idea. There are many things in the mind of the proprietor and many goals too. Particular objectives are set out in the arrangements alongside the exercises to be done to accomplish the objectives. Subsequently, planning is intentional. Planning has no significance unless it adds to the accomplishment of foreordained hierarchical objectives.

(ii) Planning is an essential capacity of administration: Planning sets out the base for different elements of administration. All other administrative capacities are performed inside the structure of the plans that are drawn by the superiors. Hence, planning goes before different capacities. This is likewise called as the power of planning. The different elements of administration are interrelated and just as critical. Therefore, planning gives the premise of every single other capacity.

(iii) Planning is pervasive: Planning is needed at all levels of administration and additionally in all branches of the association. It is not a selective capacity of top administration or of any specific office. In any case, the extent of planning contrasts at distinctive levels and among diverse divisions. For instance, the top administration plans for the whole organization, the central administration ensures that all the departments do the work. Administrators finish at the most minimal level or operational level planning.

(iv) Planning is consistent: Plans are readied for a particular timeframe, may be for a month, a quarter, or a year. Toward the end of that period there is requirement for another arrangement to be drawn on the premise of new prerequisites and future conditions. Subsequently, Planning is a consistent procedure. Congruity of Planning is connected with the Planning cycle. It implies that an arrangement is drawn up; it is executed, and is trailed by another arrangement, etc.

(v) Planning is advanced: Planning basically includes looking ahead and getting ready for what's to come. The motivation behind planning is to meet future occasions adequately to the best point of preference of an association. It infers peeping into the future, examining it and foreseeing it. Planning is, along these lines, viewed as a forward looking capacity in light of estimating. Through gauging, future occasions and conditions are expected and plans are drawn. In this manner, for instance, expectation of sales is the premises on which a business firm readies its yearly arrangement for production and marketing.

(vi) Planning includes choice making: Planning basically includes decision making from among different choices and exercises. If there is one conceivable objective or a conceivable way of action, there is no requirement for planning in light of the fact that there is no decision. The requirement for planning emerges just when choices are accessible. In genuine work, planning presupposes the presence of choices. Planning, in this way, includes careful examination and assessment of every option and picking the most suitable one.

(vii) Planning requires intelligence: Planning obliges utilization of the psyche including premonition, clever creative energy and making sound decisions.

Constraints of Planning

We have perceived how planning is crucial for business associations. It is hard to oversee operations without formal planning. It is essential for an association to move towards accomplishing objectives. However, we have frequently found in our everyday lives additionally, that things don't generally work out as expected. Unexpected occasions and changes, ascend in expenses and costs, natural changes, government mediations, lawful regulations, all influence our marketable strategies. Plans then should be adjusted. On the off chance that we can't stick to our arrangements, then why not plan anew to make sure that we can adjust to the situation, as required. The constraints of planning are:

(i) Planning prompts inflexibility: In an association, a very characterized arrangement is drawn up with particular objectives to be accomplished inside of a particular time period. These arrangements then choose the future game plan and supervisors may not be in a position to change it. This sort of unbending nature in arrangements may make trouble. Managers should be given some adaptability to have the capacity to adapt to the changed circumstances. Taking after a pre-chosen arrangement, when circumstances have changed, may not end up being in the association's interest.

(ii) Planning May not work in a dynamic situation: The business environment is dynamic, nothing is steady. The environment comprises of various measurements, monetary, political, physical, legislative and social measurements. The association needs to always adjust to changes. It gets to be hard to precisely survey future patterns in the world if monetary approaches are changed or political conditions in the nation are not steady or there is an economical catastrophe. Rivalry in the business sector can likewise disturb monetary arrangements, sales targets might be overhauled and, appropriately, money-spending plans additionally should be adjusted since they depend on sales figures. Planning can't anticipate everything and in this way, there may be impediments to successful planning.

(iii) Planning diminishes inventiveness: Planning is an action that is finished by the top administration. Typically there is not a lot of work left after the top management has made the plans. As a result, only the top managers make decisions and other managers are neither permitted to go astray from arrangements nor are they allowed to follow up on their own. Along these lines, a great part of the activity or inventiveness inborn in them likewise gets lost or diminished. More often than not, workers don't even endeavor to figure arranges. They just do what is ordered. In this way, Planning in a manner lessens imagination since individuals tend to think similarly as others.

(iv) Planning includes tremendous expenses: When arrangements are drawn up colossal expenses is included in their definition. These may require a lot of time and cash for instance; checking precision of realities may include wasting of time. Precise arrangements require logical estimations to find out raw numbers. The expenses caused some of the time may not legitimize the advantages got from the arrangements. There are various accidental expenses also, similar to costs on meeting room gatherings, dialogs with expert specialists and preparatory examinations to figure out the arrangement's practicality.

(v) Planning is a period devouring procedure: Sometimes plans take so much time to be drawn up that it takes such a large amount of time that there is very little time left for their usage.

(vi) Planning does not ensure achievement: The accomplishment of an undertaking is conceivable just when arrangements are legitimately drawn up and executed. Any arrangement should be deciphered without hesitation or it gets to be unimportant. Managers tend to depend on already attempted and tried fruitful arrangements. If the plans are not really new, then they might fail again. Using the same plans over and over again only leads to lack of incentive by even the work force.

Planning Process

Planning, as we all know is choosing ahead of time what to and how to do. It is a procedure of choice making. How would we go about making an arrangement? Since Planning is an action there are sure consistent steps for each director to use.

(i) Setting Objectives: As a matter of first importance. The first step is setting targets. Each association must have certain goals. Objectives may be set for the whole association and every office or unit inside of the association. Targets or objectives indicate what the association needs to accomplish. It could mean an increment in deals by 30 percent, which could be target of the whole association. Goals ought to be expressed unmistakably for all divisions, units and representatives. They provide guidance to all divisions. Divisions/units then need to set their own particular goals inside of the expansive structure of the association's indicated goals. Goals need to permeate down to every unit and workers at all levels. In the meantime, directors must contribute thoughts and partake in the target setting procedure. They should likewise see how their activities add to accomplishing destinations. On the off chance that the deciding results are clear it gets to be simpler to work towards the objective.

(ii) Developing Premises: Planning is related with the future which is indeterminate and each organization make its own assumption about what may happen in future. Hence, the manager is obliged to make certain assumptions about what's to come. These assumptions are called premises. Presumptions are the base material whereupon arrangements are to be drawn. The base material may be as gauges, existing arrangements or any past data about strategies. The premises must be the same for all and there ought to add up to concurrence on them. All administrators included in planning ought to be acquainted with and utilizing the same assumptions. For case, looking into the future is imperative in creating premises, as it is a procedure of social event data. Figures can be made about the interest for a specific item, approach change, interest rates, and costs of capital merchandise, duty rates and so forth. Exact estimates; thus get to be vital for fruitful arrangements.

(iii) Identifying options: Once targets are set, goals are made; it is time to look into the various options. At that point the following step would be to follow up on them. There may be numerous approaches to act and accomplish targets. All the options ought to be distinguished. The way of action that may be taken could be either standard or imaginative. Including more individuals and sharing their thoughts may embrace a creative course. On the off chance that the venture is imperative, then more options ought to be created and completely talked about amongst the individuals from the association.

(iv) Evaluating the options: The following step is to measure the advantages and disadvantages of every option. Every course will have numerous variables that must be weighed against one another. The positive and negative parts of every proposition should be assessed in the target's light to be accomplished. In money related arrangements, for instance, the negative return exchange off is exceptionally regular. The more hazardous the venture, the higher the profits it is liable to give. Precise assumptions in states of sureness/vulnerability then get to be essential presumptions for these propositions. Choices are assessed in the light of their possibility and end results.

(v) Selecting an option: This is the genuine purpose of choice making. The best arrangement must be received and actualized. The perfect arrangement, obviously, would be the most practical, beneficial and with minimum negative outcomes. Most arranges may not generally be subjected to a numerical investigation. In such cases, subjectivity and the manager's experience, judgment and now and again, instinct have critical impact in selecting the most suitable option. Some of the time, a mix of arrangements may be chosen rather than one best course. The director will need to apply changes and mixes and select the best conceivable strategy.

(vi) Implementing the arrangement: This is the step where other administrative capacities come into the photo. It is related with completing the arrangement without hesitation i.e., doing what is needed. For instance, if there is an arrangement to expand the business then more workers, more resources will be needed, and for which plans would have to be made.

Doesn't the term "project management" sound like a big deal? It sure does. Project managers can come from different fields. In real estate, they could be engineers or architects. In advertising, they could be people from marketing or graphics design. In schools, they could be educators and administrators. People from different backgrounds and qualifications can spearhead projects as long as they have the skill to plan, organize, implement, and evaluate a task or project.

Project management is a process used to solve problems or achieve specific goals. Although the contexts and scales by which it can be used may differ, the idea is one and the same: *get things done.*

This book is a practical guide to project management, so it means that you get a chance to practice what you learn, and we will start with the first step: planning.

Planning is the first step to project management because it prepares your roadmap to success. Good projects start with good plans. Having a plan has several advantages:

1. *It keeps you focused on what you need to do.* Planning helps you prioritize key areas of concern. Even when there are many things that you need to coordinate, a well-done plan will help keep you on track and ensures your steady progress to project completion.

2. *It makes teamwork easy.* More than just one person often does project management, so teamwork is necessary. A plan enables the team to harmoniously coordinate. In other words, it ensures that you and your team are on the same page.

3. *It gives you confidence.* No matter how complicated things may seem and no matter how much work needs to be done, you will have certainty that you can achieve it because you have a plan in place. This confidence will help you make better decisions as you go about project management.

Having briefly discussed the importance and advantages of planning in the context of project management, let us now proceed to the first step in crafting a plan: identifying goals.

Identifying a Project's Specific Goals

There could be nothing worse in project management than having no clue as to what it is that you need to do, or what it is that's expected from you. The goal is the first thing you need to have in mind when creating a plan. You need to write down the goal. You need to fully understand what it means and what it will take to get it done.

A goal should be SMART:

1. Specific - a goal should be easy to target and explain. It at least identifies the who, what, when, where and why of the project.

2. Measurable – you need to be able to measure or quantify success in the achievement of this goal.

3. Achievable – although goals can be challenging, they have to be realistic enough to help give you a shot at success.

4. Relevant – you need to understand the importance of this goal, or at least, its relevance to you and your community.

5. Time-bound – you need to have a target date for the completion of your project.

Challenge

Let's say that you work for a huge bookstore company and you happen to be the director for CSR (corporate social responsibility) projects. You were given a task to hold a Book Fair event within your company's vicinity that will encourage parents and children to read books together, and at the same time, obtain book or cash donations for your company's chosen orphanage.

There are already several useful details given in the statement above, but this goal may not necessarily be *SMART* just yet. Although this example is hypothetical, could you make this goal specific, measurable, achievable, realistic and timely?

Give it a try and write down how this SMART goal should look like:

_____
_____
_____
_____.

Your choice of words and structure may be different but you have learned what *SMART* means if you gave an answer like "The goal of this project is for the CSR Team to hold a book fair in the month of August at the company lobby, and obtain at least 1000 books via cash or book donation, to be given to Care for Children Orphanage in October this year."

Note that while you have a main vision, mission or goal, you may also have some supporting goals or sub-goals in mind. For instance, if the main goal is to raise book reading habits in various households within the community, a sub-goal of the project could be holding book fairs and other similar events.

Creating a Project Schedule

Now that you have a goal, it's time for you to plan on ways to achieve it. By now, you probably understand that in planning a project, you need to be able to define exactly what the project is all about so you could write a SMART goal and create a project schedule based on that goal.

What is a project schedule? A project schedule outlines tasks to be accomplished in order to make your goal achievable. This will serve as your primary monitoring and reporting tool to help guide you in the key areas of your deliverables.

A good schedule allows you to make realistic estimates as to your project's overall budget and enables you to predict if there are any adjustments that need to be made it, and how these adjustments will affect your deadlines, finances, resources and expectations.

In order to come up with a project schedule, you need to have these basic elements:

1. List of specific tasks – Tasks can be main tasks or supporting tasks. Main tasks have a huge contribution to the fulfillment of your goal, whereas supporting tasks are items that need to be done in order to help accomplish a main task.

    a. *Question:* If, for instance, the main task is to "create marketing and advertising materials for the event," what will your supporting tasks be?

    b. *Answer:* Supporting tasks may include obtaining the budget for the materials, design and approval of posters, brochures and online collaterals, delivery of the materials and finally, the posting and distribution of these materials.

2. Task Duration and Deadline – Task duration lets you know how much time is dedicated to a completion of a certain task, while the deadline specifies the date of the task's completion.

    a. *Question:* If, for instance, the main task is to "create marketing and advertising materials for the event," what possible task duration and deadline can be set?

b. *Answer:* Task duration can indicate one month, like June 1-July 1, 2015. Meanwhile, the deadline can be set on July 1, 2015.

3. Persons responsible – one of the most important things that need to be established when you are engaged in project management, is obtaining your team's accountability to the tasks they are assigned to. You are likely to be most effective if you have a point person for each and every task and sub-task that you have indicated. This way, you know which person to call and follow-up on the tasks that you have on your schedule. You will know from whom you can expect reports to come in and when.

4. Communications: Documentation/Reporting required – this section of your project plan indicates reports given to the stakeholders and the persons in-charge of information. Once a "person responsible completes a task" it is the duty of this person to communicate progress to a project leader or stakeholder. If there are problems met and adjustments are needed to be made in terms of the deadline or budget in relation to a particular task, reporting should also be

required. Remember that effective communication is one of the secret keys to a project's success.

   a. *Question:* If the person responsible for "creating marketing and advertising materials for the event," is assigned to the Marketing Officer and Advertising Manager of the company, what documentation or reporting is required from them to submit?

   b. *Answer:* The marketing officer and advertising manager can submit the finished samples of marketing and advertising materials to the project management leader, the CEO and possible sponsors and co-sponsors of the event.

5. Budget – no project can be made possible without setting a realistic budget. You need to find out where the money and resources are coming from, what items need to be bought, what services need to be outsourced and when the payments will be due. It is useful to integrate the budget to your project schedule, but if you can have a person in your team to be assigned the role of project accountant or accounts officer, having a separate paper showing only the budget forecast will be useful, too.

Konrad Obidoski

Chapter 6

Different Types of Plans

There are various types of plans that you can pick from and it is up to you to decide if you want to implement all of them or only a few. These plans would supplement in the success of your organization.

In light of what the proposed plan looks to accomplish and the technique, which the plan might want to receive, they can be delegated into segments— Goals, Strategy, Policy, Procedure, Method, Rule, Program, and Budget.

Goals

The initial phase in organizing is setting goals. Targets, in this way, can be said to be the wanted future position that the administration might want to reach. Targets are extremely essential to the association and they are characterized as results that the administration tries to accomplish by its operations. Thusly, a target basically expressed is the thing that you might want to accomplish, i.e., the absolute end result of exercises. For instance, an association may have a target of expanding deals by 10% or acquiring a sensible rate of rate of profitability, win a 20% benefit from business. They denote the desired result of the organizing process. All other administrative exercises are likewise coordinated towards accomplishing these objectives. They are normally set by top administration of the association and are focused on expansive, general issues. They characterize the future situation that the association endeavors to figure out. They serve as an aide for general business arranging. Diverse divisions or units in the organization may have their own objectives. Goals or objectives should be communicated in particular terms i.e., they ought to be quantifiable in quantitative terms, as a composed articulation of wanted results to be accomplished inside of a given time period.

Strategy

A strategy gives the expansive shapes of an association's business. It will likewise allude to future choices characterizing the associations heading and extension over the long haul. Hence, we can say a system is an exhaustive arrangement for fulfilling objectives of an organization. This thorough arrangement will incorporate three measurements,

- Estimating long-term goals

- Receiving a specific game-plan, and

- Allotting assets important to accomplish the goal

Whenever a strategy is formulated, the business environment should be mulled over. The adjustments in the financial, political, social, lawful and mechanical environment will influence an association's technique. Strategies normally take the course of framing the associations personality in the business environment. Major decisions will incorporate choices like whether the association will keep on being in the same line of business, or join new lines of movement with the current business or look to get a predominant position in the same business sector. For instance, an organization's showcasing system needs to address certain inquiries i.e., who are the clients? What is the interest for the item? Which channel of appropriation to utilize? What is the evaluating approach? What's more? How would we promote the item? These and numerous more issues should be determined while figuring a strategy for any association.

Policy

Policies are general explanations that guide thinking or channelize energies towards a specific bearing. Policies give a premise to translating strategies that are typically expressed as general terms. They are advisers for administrative activity and choices in the usage of methodology. For instance, the organization may have an enrollment approach, evaluating strategy inside which goals are set and choices are made. On the off chance that there is a set up strategy, it gets to be simpler to determine issues or problems. Hence, a policy is the general reaction to a specific issue or circumstance.

There are approaches for all levels and divisions in the association extending from significant organization strategies to minor arrangements. Real organization plans are for all to know i.e., clients, customers, contenders and so forth, though minor polices are pertinent to insiders and contain moment points of interest of data crucial to the workers of an association. Be that as it may, there must be a few prerequisites and rules for revealing data to others.

Policies characterize the wide parameters inside which a supervisor may work. The director may utilize his/her circumspection to decipher and apply a strategy. For instance, the decisions taken under a Purchase Policy would be in the way of assembling or purchasing choices. Should an organization make or purchase its necessities of bundles, transport administrations, printing of stationery, water and power supply and different things? By what method ought to merchants be chosen for acquiring supplies? What number of suppliers ought to an organization make buys from? What is the criterion for picking suppliers? The Purchase Policy would tend to every one of these answers.

Procedure

Procedures are normal strides on the most proficient method to complete exercises. They detail the definite way in which any work is to be performed. They are designated in a sequential order, chronological in almost all cases. For instance, there may be a method for ordering supplies before generation. Procedures are determined steps to be followed in a proper order. They are for the most part implied for insiders to take after. The grouping of steps or moves to be made is to uphold an approach and to accomplish pre-decided destinations. Policies and procedure, hence, are closely interlinked. Procedures are ventures to be carried out inside of an expansive policy structure.

Method

Methods give the appropriate way in which an undertaking must be performed considering the target. It manages an assignment containing one stage of a system and determines how this stride is to be performed. Methods may shift from assignment to assignment. Determination of fitting technique spares time, cash and exertion and builds effectiveness. For granting training to representatives at different level from top administration to supervisory, distinctive routines can be received. For instance for more elevated amount administration introduction projects, addresses and workshops can be sorted out while at the supervisory level, at work preparing systems and work-arranged routines are suitable.

Rules

Standards or rules are particular proclamations that educate employees about what anyone is at the capacity of doing. They don't take into account any adaptability or prudence. It mirrors an administrative choice that a sure action must or must not be taken. They are generally the least difficult kind of arrangements in light of the fact that there is no trade off or change unless a strategy choice is taken.

Programme

Programmes are itemized proclamations around an undertaking that diagrams the targets, approaches, systems, standards, assignments, human and physical assets obliged and the financial backing to actualize any game plan. Programmes will incorporate the whole array of exercises and also the association's approach and how it will add to the general strategy for success. The minutest points of interest are worked out i.e., systems, tenets, spending plans, inside of the wide approach structure.

Budget

A financial plan or budget is an announcement of expected results communicated in numerical terms. It is a plan that measures future numbers. For instance, a business-spending plan may conjecture the offers of diverse items in every range for a specific month. A financial plan might likewise be arranged to demonstrate the quantity of laborers needed in the processing plant at top generation times. Since a spending plan represents all things in numbers, it is simpler to contrast real figures and expected figures and make restorative move in this manner. Subsequently, a financial plan is likewise a control gadget from which deviations can be dealt with. However, making a financial plan includes gauging and informed predictions, in this manner, it obviously goes under planning. It is a principal planning device in numerous associations. Take the example of Cash Budget. The cash budget is an essential apparatus in the administration of money. It is a gadget to help the administration to arrange and control the utilization of money. It is an announcement demonstrating the assessed money inflows and money surges over a given period. Money inflows would by and large originate from money deals and the money surges would for the most part be the expenses and costs connected with the business' operations. The net money position is dictated by the money spending plan i.e., inflows minus (–) outpourings = surplus or lack.

The administration needs to hold satisfactory financial balance for different purposes. Be that as it may, in the meantime, it ought to keep away from abundance equalization of money since it gives next to zero return. The business needs to evaluate and arrange its requirement for money with a level of precision and caution.

Project Planning Tips

1. *Have brainstorming sessions.* How do you ensure that you are creating an effective project schedule? Dedicate some time to have *brainstorming sessions* with your team. Have an outline of tasks and deadlines written prior to your meeting or brainstorming sessions so that you can effectively initiate the discussion. At the same time, obtain additional comments, tasks or suggestions from your team.

2. *Draw it, show it!* Another good way to create an effective project schedule is to create some kind of *illustrative road map* to indicate your general tasks. This is a creative way to go about your planning as some people can be more "visual" and more easily remember drawings than words

on paper. This is a good way to start your plan before you list all the details down in words on paper.

3. *Write it down.* You may create your own project schedule format on a Word document or Excel spreadsheet. You may even use a downloadable Gantt chart to aid your project schedule. Whatever format it is that you want to use, prioritize the format that you can easily *understand, refer to and share with your team.*

4. *Discuss your project schedule/plan.* No matter how well written your plan is, it will be useless unless your team understands what it is all about. Once you have finalized your project schedule, go over it with your team and ensure that they understand every detail.

5. *Schedule periodic evaluations.* Be sure to include *periodic evaluation meetings* in your project schedule, say every two or three weeks, to help keep yourself updated on your team's progress. This will also help your team easily celebrate milestones – big tasks that you have accomplished or interesting developments you have made for the project.

Chapter Summary

In summary, this chapter has enabled you to

- Identify a project's specific goals – create a project goal that is specific, measurable, achievable, relevant and time-bound.

- Create a project schedule – come up with a project schedule that includes tasks, duration and deadlines, persons responsible, documentation and budget.

- Obtain tips on project planning – brainstorm, draw, write and discuss your project plans. Schedule periodic evaluations to ensure that your team is making progress.

So what comes next after plans for a project have been made? The process is called project implementation. Find out all you need to know about implementing a successful project in Chapter 2.

Chapter 7

Implementing a Successful Project

When you start to implement any plan the first step is to ensure that your business does not face any dangers. You need to evaluate the cautionary measures that can be taken in case some sort of change in the environment in which you do business leads to problems in terms of doing a project. The world is ever changing and change in even a small factor can lead to problems for the business. Hence, the first step is to ensure that your firm is aware of its business environment and is keeping an eye on any changes that might take place in it.

Business Environment

The term 'business environment' implies the sum of all people, organizations and different powers that are outside the control of a business undertaking yet that may influence its execution. Accordingly, the monetary, social, political, mechanical and different dimensions that work outside a business undertaking are a piece of its surroundings. So additionally, the individual buyers or contending endeavors and in addition the administrations, shopper bunches, rivals, courts, media and different organizations working outside a venture constitute its surroundings. The essential point is that these people, foundations and powers are prone to impact the execution of a business venture despite the fact that they happen to exist outside its limits. For instance, changes in government's monetary strategies, quick innovative advancements, political vulnerability, changes in designs and tastes of customers and expanded rivalry in the business sector — all impact the working of a business undertaking in vital ways. Increment in taxes by government can make things costly to purchase. Advancement in technology may render existing items old. Political vulnerability may make dread in the psyches of capitalists and investors. Changes in styles and tastes of purchasers may change in the business sector from existing items to new ones. Expanded rivalry in the business sector may lessen net revenues of firms. On the earlier stated premises, it can be said business environment, has the accompanying elements:

(i) Totality of outer powers: Business environment is the entirety of things that are outside the control of a business firm and, all things considered, is aggregative in nature.

(ii) Specific and general powers: Business environment incorporates both particular and general powers. Particular powers, (for example, financial specialists, clients, contenders and suppliers) influence individual endeavors straightforwardly and promptly in their everyday working. General strengths, (for example, social, political, lawful and innovative conditions) have a sway on all business endeavors and along these lines may influence an individual firm just indirectly.

(iii) Inter-relatedness: Different components or parts of business environment are firmly related. For instance, expanded age expectation of individuals and expanded mindfulness for medicinal services have expanded the interest for some wellbeing items instead of unhealthy items and things like eating routine junk food, without fat cooking oil, and creation of wellbeing resorts. New wellbeing items and changes have changed individuals' ways of life.

(iv) Dynamic nature: Business environment is alterable in that it continues changing whether as far as innovative change, shifts in shopper inclinations or appearance of new rivalry in the business sector.

(v) Uncertainty: Business environment is to a great extent dubious as it is exceptionally hard to foresee future happenings, particularly when environment changes are occurring very fast and it is difficult to keep track of all the changes that are taking place simultaneously.

(vi) Complexity: Since business environment comprises of various interrelated and elemental conditions or dimensions which emerge from diverse sources, it is hard to grasp what precisely constitutes a given environment change. As such, environment is a complex phenomenon that is moderately less demanding to comprehend in parts however hard to handle in its totality. For instance, it might be hard to know the relative's degree effect of the social, monetary, political, mechanical or legitimate elements on change sought after of an item in the business sector.

(vii) Relativity: Business environment is a relative idea since it contrasts from nation to nation and even area to locale. This is because the political conditions say in Israel are pretty different from those exiting in Australia or Argentina, while the demand for a certain good might be high in one country but is hardly sough after in another country.

Significance of Business Environment

This section explains why you need to look into the changing business environment. It is not that easy to understand business environment, in fact, you may not even realize that your project is staggering because of changing in business environment, as you never bothered to understand it. This is especially true for small business enterprises that don't really look into business environment and are thwarted by larger firms.

Much the same as individuals, business endeavors don't exist in disconnection. Every business firm isn't an island in itself. The business exists, survives and develops inside of the component's setting and powers of its surroundings. While an individual firm cannot effect the business environment on its own, it can though in addition to the effect created by other organizations lead to a change in the business environment. A decent comprehension of environment by business managers enables them to recognize and assess, as well as to respond to the changes outside to their organizations. The significance of business environment and its comprehension by managers can be acknowledged on the off chance that we consider the accompanying realities:

(i) It empowers the firm to distinguish opportunities and getting the first mover point of interest: Opportunities keep on appearing in front of a firm because of the way that the business environment keeps on changing. Environment gives various chances to business achievement. Early distinguishing of opportunities helps an endeavor to be the first to adventure them as opposed to losing them to contenders. For instance, there are many companies that benefit from selling their product to emerging economies because they understand that these countries have low-income class citizens who like to buy products that are not high in quality but simply are cheaper.

(ii) It assists the firm to recognize dangers and early danger signs: Threats allude to the outside environment patterns and changes that will block a company's execution. Other than circumstances, environment happens to be the wellspring of numerous dangers. Natural mindfulness by managers can help supervisors to distinguish different dangers on time and serve as an early cautioning sigh. For instance, many emerging economies are plagued by something known as FDI (Foreign Direct Investment). The foreign companies try to enter the market of developing nations and try to hijack their development. In this way the country itself cannot benefit because its own local firms stop to grow. Hence, change in the business environment can help the firm to realize the fact that another company might be entering the market and for that purpose changes have to be made.

(iii) It helps in tapping valuable assets: Environment is a wellspring of different assets for maintaining a business. To take part in an action, a business venture gathers different assets called inputs like fund, machines, crude materials, power and water, work, and so on, from its surroundings including customers, government agents and suppliers. They choose to use these assets for their own particular desires to receive something consequently for doing business. The business endeavor supplies the society with its yields, for example, merchandise and administrations for clients, installment of assessments to government, return on budgetary speculation to financial specialists, etc. Since the undertaking relies upon nature as a wellspring of inputs or assets as an outlet for yields, it just bodes well that the endeavor outlines arrangements that permit it to get the assets that it needs so it can change over those assets into yields that the society wants. This should be possible better by comprehending what are the needs of the society.

(iv) It assists in adapting quickly to changes: Today's business ventures are getting progressively alert where changes are occurring at a quick pace. It is not the actuality of progress itself that is as essential as the pace of progress. Turbulent economic situations, less brand dependability, divisions and sub-divisions (fracture) of business sectors, all the more requesting clients, fast changes in innovation and exceptional worldwide rivalry are only a couple of examples used depict today's business surroundings. All sizes of businesses and a wide range of endeavors are confronting each other progressively in this dynamic environment. Keeping in mind the end goal to adequately adapt to these huge changes, directors must comprehend and look at the society and create suitable game plans.

(v) It helps in Planning: Since environment is a wellspring of both internal and external dangers for a business undertaking, its comprehension and examination can be the premise for choosing the future game-plan or preparing rules for choice making. For instance, if there is the entry of a new rival in the business environment, the business has to take suitable actions to ensure that its profits do not diminish.

(vi) It helps in enhancing execution: The last explanation behind comprehending business environment identifies whether it truly has any kind of effect in the execution of an endeavor. The answer is that it seems to have many kinds of effect. Numerous studies uncover that the fate of an undertaking is firmly bound up with what is occurring in the world. What's more, the ventures that constantly screen their surroundings and embrace suitable business practices are the ones which enhance their present execution as well as keep on succeeding in the business sector for a more extended period.

Measurements of Business Environment

There are various types of changes that take place in a business environment. You obviously cannot look into each and every one of these changes and hence, this part will divide them for you so that you can make a chart where you can record all the changes taking place in the business environment.

Measurements of, or the components constituting the business environment incorporate financial, social, innovative, and political and law related conditions that are viewed as significant for choice making and enhancing the execution of an undertaking. Rather than the particular environment, these elements clarify the general environment, which for the most part impacts numerous ventures in the meantime. On the other hand, administration of each venture can profit by being mindful of these measurements as opposed to being unaware about them.

(i) Economic Environment: Interest rates, expansion rates, changes in extra income of individuals, securities exchange records and the estimation of currency are a portion of the financial elements that can influence administration changes in a business endeavor. Short and long term interest rates altogether influence the interest for an item and its administrations. For instance, if there is a firm that it starts raising its production of cars then its sales might increase even more if the interest rates on care loans were very less. This is because such things induce the customer to buy more something as they have to play less and the interest rate may rise in the future. Likewise, an increase in the salary of individuals because of expansion in the total national output of a nation ensures that more and more people would start buying high quality luxury goods. High expansion rates for the most part result in imperatives on business endeavors as they expand the different expenses of business, for example, the cost of crude materials that are used for production or hardware.

Segments of Economic Environment

- Existing structure of the economy, as far as relative part of private and open segments.

- The rates of development of GNP and per capita income at present and consistent costs

- Rates of sparing and speculation

- Volume of imports and fares of diverse things

- Balance of installments and changes in outside trade rates

- Agricultural and modern generation patterns

- Expansion of transportation and correspondence offices

- Money supply in the economy

- Public obligation towards buying of products

- Planned expense in private and open segments

(ii) Social Environment: The social environment of business incorporate the social strengths like traditions and customs, values, social patterns, society's desires from business, and so on. Customs characterize social practices that have gone on for a considerable length of time or even hundreds of years. For instance, there are many regional festivals that are carried out in every country that give an opportunity to all the ventures to increase their sales by marketing and selling products that are specific to the needs of that festival. Quality is something that that general public holds in high regard. In most countries, singular flexibility, social equity, fairness of chance and national mix are cases of real values treasured by all the citizens of that particular nation. This is why a business has to keep in mind the culture of every nation before they begin setting up their venture. In business terms, these qualities decipher into opportunity of decision in the business sector, business' obligation towards the general public and non-biased vocation rehearses. Social patterns present different opportunities as well as dangers to business ventures. For instance, the wellbeing and-wellness pattern has gotten to be prevalent among substantial number of urban inhabitants. This has made an interest for items like natural nourishment; eating fewer carbohydrates, less consumption of soda pops, exercise centers, packaged water and sustenance supplements. This pattern has, then again, hurt business in different commercial enterprises like dairy handling, tobacco and alcohol.

Significant Elements of Social Environment

- Attitudes towards item developments, ways of life, word related dispersion and customer inclinations

- Concern with personal satisfaction

- Life hope

- Expectations from the workforce

- Shifts in the vicinity of female employees in the workforce

- Birth and demise rates

- Population shifts

- Educational framework and education rates

- Consumption propensities

- Composition of the employees

(iii) Technological Environment: Technological environment incorporates powers identifying with innovative enhancements and advancements which give better approaches for delivering products and administrations and new strategies and systems of working a business. For instance, late mechanical, progresses in PCs and gadgets have changed the courses in which organizations publicize their items. It is common now to see flash drives instead of things like floppy's or CD's, modernized data booths, and interactive media pages highlighting the ethics of items on the Internet. Likewise, retailers have direct connections with suppliers who renew stocks when required. Producers have adaptable assembling frameworks. Aircraft organizations have Internet pages where clients can search for flight times, destinations and passages and book their tickets on the web. Likewise, proceeding with advancements in diverse experimental and building fields, for example, lasers, applied autonomy, biotechnology, sustenance additives, drug, telecom and engineered fills have given various open doors and dangers to a wide range of undertakings. Shifting from popular devices like vacuum tubes to transistors, from steam trains to diesel and electric motors, from wellspring pens to ballpoint, from propeller planes to flies, and from typewriters to PC based word processors, have all been mindful and have created new opportunities for all the firms.

(iv) Political Environment: Political environment incorporates political conditions, for example, general steadiness and peace in the nation and particular mentalities that chose government agents viewpoint towards business. The essentialness of political conditions in business achievement lies in the consistency of business exercises under stable political conditions. Then again, there may be instability of business exercises because of political turmoil and dangers to peace. Political steadiness, along these lines, develops certainty among businessmen to put resources into the long haul ventures for the economy's development. Political shakiness can change that certainty. Essentially, the mentalities of government authorities towards business may have either positive or negative effect upon business. For instance, there are some economies that never opened their gates to the worldwide economy. In the long run, all of these economies suffered because they were not able to get the required resources and income to sustain their growth and survival. The amount of money that is generated if an economy is open to the world is way more than one that is closed. Hence, the government outlook can change the status of the economy of a country by just opening their doors to the world.

Significant Elements of Political Environment

- The nation's legal requirement

- Prevailing political framework

- The level of politicization of business and financial issues

- Dominant belief systems and estimations of major political gatherings

- The nature and profile of political authority and considering political identities

- The level of political ethical quality

- Political organizations like the administration and associated offices

- Political philosophy and practices of the decision party

- The degree and nature of government intercession in business

- The nature of relationship of a nation with outside nations

(v) Legal Environment: Legal environment incorporates different enactments authorized by the Government agencies and requests issued by government powers, court judgments and the choices rendered by different commissions and offices at each level of the administration—main, state or local. It is necessary for the administration of each endeavor to comply with the rules that have been laid down by the government. Along these lines, a satisfactory learning of tenets and regulations surrounded by the Government is a pre-imperative for better business execution. Resistance of laws can arrive the business undertaking into legitimate issues. Effect of legislative environment can be shown with the assistance of government regulations to secure shopper's hobbies. For instance, the notice of mixed drinks is precluded. Ads, including parcels of cigarettes convey the statutory cautioning 'Cigarette smoking is damaging to wellbeing'. Additionally, ads of infant nourishment should essentially educate the potential purchaser that mother's milk is the best. Every one of these regulation that have to be followed by every business organization, if a business organization wants to be successful in another country then it has to go over all the regulations and make sure that they comply to them. It can be difficult to understand the laws of another country and there are many cases where firms were not able to comply with the necessary legal requirements because they were unfamiliar with the laws.

Konrad Obidoski

Chapter 8

Organizing

When implementing the plan, organizing is very important. This process basically decides how you will do something. It makes sure that everything is available for the completion of the project. Hence, when implementing the plan, organizing is also very important.

Let us take a look at the organizing process. Have you ever paid consideration to how, the school fete that you appreciate so much really happens? What goes ahead behind the scene to make it the success you desire and so enjoy? The entire movement is separated into task forces, each in charge of managing a particular region like the sustenance board of trustees, the decorations advisory group, the ticketing panel et cetera. These are under the general supervision of the officials responsible for the occasion.

Planning connections are built up among the different gatherings to enable smooth communication and clarity regarding every council's commitment towards the occasion. All the above exercises are an organizing function each. Organizing basically infers a procedure which comprises of coordinating human endeavors, amasses assets and incorporating both into a combined effort to be used for accomplishing indicated goals. Organizing can be characterized as a procedure that starts implementation of arrangements by delegating roles and working connections and successfully sending assets for achievement of recognized and craved results (objectives).

The Process of Organizing

Organizing includes a progression of steps that should be taken keeping in mind the end goal to accomplish the wanted objective. Let us take a look at how getting organized is accomplished with the assistance of an illustration. Assume twelve students work for the school library in the late spring getaways. One evening they are advised to empty a shipment of new books, stock the bookshelves, and afterward discard all waste (bundling, paper and so on). On the off chance that every one of them chooses to do it in their own specific manner, it will bring about absolute disarray. Be that as it may, if one of them oversees the work by regrouping, separating the work, delegating each individual's quota of work and creating a working relationship among them, the work will be done speedier and in a more efficient way. Going by this example, the following steps constitute the process of organizing:

(i) **Identification and division of work**: The initial phase during the time spent organizing includes distinguishing and distributing the work that must be done as per the constraints. The work is isolated into easier exercises such that duplication can occur effectively.

(ii) **Departmentalization**: Once work has been isolated into smaller exercises then those exercises that are close in nature are gathered together. Such sets encourage specialization. This gathering procedure is called departmentalization. Divisions can be made utilizing a few criteria as a premise. Some examples of the most prevalently utilized premise are region (north, south, west and so forth.) and items (apparatuses, garments, makeup and so forth).

(iii) **Delegating duties**: It is important to allot work to different representatives. When departments have been shaped, each of them is set under the charge of a person. Jobs are then apportioned to the individuals from every segment in understanding to their aptitudes and capabilities. It is crucial for effective performance that a legitimate match is made between the way of a vocation and the capacity of a person. The work must be relegated to the individuals who have the capacity to perform it well.

(iv) **Establishing leadership roles**: Merely dispensing work is not enough. Every individual ought to know who he needs to take orders from and to whom he is responsible. The foundation of such clear connections serves to make a hierarchal structure and aides in coordination amongst different divisions.

Significance of Organizing

Execution of the organizing capacity can enable a smooth move of the enterprise keeping in mind the dynamic business environment. The importance of organizing for the most part emerges from the way that it helps in the survival and development of an endeavor and prepares it to meet different obstacles and overcome them. All together for any business venture to perform jobs and effectively meet objectives, the organizing capacity must be appropriately performed. The following points highlight the pivotal part that organizing plays in any business undertaking:

(i) **Benefits of specialization**: Organizing prompts an efficient portion of occupations amongst the work power. This lessens the workload and in addition upgrades profitability as a result of specialists performing a part of the job at a given time. Continuous and repetitive execution of a specific assignment enables a worker to pick up involvement here and prompts specialization.

(ii) **Clarity in working connections**: The foundation of working connections elucidates lines of correspondence and determines who is to answer to whom. This eliminates the problem of vagueness in exchange of data and guidelines. It helps in establishing an order of hierarchy to be followed, thus allocating responsibility and limiting and outlining the extent of authority to be exercised by an individual.

(iii) **Optimum use of assets**: Organizing ensures the best possible use of all material, finances and human resources at disposal. Appropriate assigning of jobs helps in avoiding the overlapping of work and furthermore makes the best utilization of assets conceivable. Avoiding duplication of work aides the minimizing the wastage of assets and endeavors.

(iv) **Adaptation to change**: The procedure of organizing permits a business endeavor to adapt to changes in the business environment. It permits the structure to be suitably altered and the change and revision amongst administrative levels to transition smoothly. It likewise gives highly required solidarity to the enterprise as it can then keeps on surviving and develop despite changes.

(v) **Effective organization**: Organizing gives a reasonable depiction of jobs and related obligations. This serves to avoid any disarray and duplication. Clarity in working connections empowers legitimate execution of work. Administration of an endeavor consequently turns out to be simple and this acquires viability in an organization.

(vi) **Development of personnel**: Organizing empowers inventiveness and creativity amongst the workers. Efficient delegation of work amongst the employees permits managers to lessen their workload by allotting routine jobs to their subordinates. The reduction in workload by is not just necessary on account of limitations of an individual- it additionally permits them to develop newer routines and methods for performing errands. It gives them an ideal opportunity to investigate territories for development and the chance to improve subsequently

(vii) **Expansion and development**: Organizing aides in the development and enhancement of an endeavor by empowering it to stray from existing standards and taking up new difficulties.

It permits a business undertaking to include more occupation positions, offices and even expand their product offerings. New land domains can be added to current ranges of operation and this will help to expand client base, deals and benefit. In this manner, getting organized is a procedure by which the manager removes strife among individuals over work or sharing responsibilities and makes a domain suitable for cooperation.

There is enough information on what the project is all about and what it wishes to accomplish. There are resources to use, there is a budget to work on and there are people to help with the project. Finally, there is also a well-written plan as to how everything can be achieved. What's next? Getting to action!

Implementing a successful project plan involves mainly two things: leadership and persistence.

Project Leadership

The best way to implement a project is to lead by example. Leadership is a process in which a leader positively influences the members of a team and moves them to action.

What is your primary role in project management? To *manage* a project means to oversee it. You are tasked with ensuring that a planned project becomes a reality. This is why you have a huge task or involvement in the course of *project planning*. Delivering a clear and well-understood project plan is one of the tasks of a project leader.

In the course of implementing a project, what responsibilities are expected from a project manager or project leader? Here are some of them.

1. Strategize - As the project is implemented, come up with a strategy to make achievement of various tasks easier, faster and more affordable. Are there tasks that can be completed before the assigned deadline? Do you know companies that can help sponsor your advertising requirements? Are there members of your team who can be assigned to do multiple tasks? In addition, consider which items you can personally do or accomplish for your team.

2. Empower – As the project manager, you need to learn to empower the different members of your team. This means that you let them feel that they are perfectly capable of accomplishing the tasks assigned to them. You let them know that they can be supported with the resources they need. They have to understand that they are authorized to make certain decisions within their scope. Just as people are accountable to ensure the success of a certain task,

they, too, are qualified to receive appropriate recognition for the accomplishment of the same.

3. Communicate – It is your primary role to listen to inquiries and developments in the project, as well as to ask questions. These apply not only to your team members but also to the project stakeholders. Always be in the know of their various expectations and issues. Always be on top of updates and recent developments in the projects. Know what the challenges are and be ready to give answers as regards how you plan to address these challenges.

4. Build and rebuild the team – Make an effort to ensure that your team works together. While each member of the team should be responsible for a specific task, the members should function as a unit and move towards the same direction, fulfilling the tasks at hand.

5. Help solve problems – try to predict possible challenges and problems before they happen. Ideally, you are the first person to come up with a "Plan B" in your team.

Being a manager and leader is a challenging role. You must be confident, passionate and knowledgeable. You must also have a good way of dealing with people of various kinds and personalities. While these characteristics may take time to fully develop, find comfort in the fact that your passion, perseverance and hard work will help you make up for whatever qualities you may lack.

Follow-ups

Notice how a child easily gets what he wants from his parents? Be it a toy or candy, a child never stops bugging his parents until he gets what he wants.

And that is why he gets it.

We may get sick and tired of people who are persistent, but you can be sure that these people get what they want. Like they say, "squeaky tires get the oil."

While you may trust team members to be held accountable for each of their responsibilities, you can also help them attend to it by following up consistently. Monitor the accomplishment of project tasks by getting updates whenever possible and asking for reports or documentation that will help show the progress that has been made in the project.

For instance, if you are monitoring your target guest visits at a book fair, follow up not only by getting the number of visitors you get per day but also try to take a look at the number of invitations you have sent to companies and other target markets.

Monitoring Accomplishments

The reason you do follow-ups on task completion is to ensure that you 1) get to monitor and record progress, and 2) apply adjustments and interventions when needed.

Monitoring accomplishments go hand in hand with doing follow-ups. Once you have reminded your team members about ensuring that a particular task is completed or finished, be sure to not only take their word for it, but to actively monitor and witness the completion of such task.

Remember the project schedule discussed in Chapter 1? Besides this project schedule that you have discussed with everyone, indicate in your own schedule some dates and times when you should follow-up on important matters within your team to ensure that things are moving forward. This means that it may also be helpful not only to follow up via phone call or email, but that you also need to take time to visit sites, work stations and project locations. This way, you will really be on top of what's happening.

Going back to the example with which you followed up on the visitors for your book fair, along with following up that more invitations are sent, try not only to find out from your team what has been done. Go to the site and take a look at the guests who visit your event. From the list of your invited guests, call up a person or two whom you know from the list and ask them if they have received the invitation you sent. Talk to them about the event. Besides giving them your personal invitation, you also become certain that your invitations have been delivered properly and on time.

Communication with Stakeholders

The previous sections focused on your relationship with your team. But another important task you are given is to ensure that your stakeholders are properly updated in the course of project implementation. Whether or not you are asked for updates, make it a priority to coordinate with your stakeholders from time to time.

Stakeholders are people who have something to expect in the project you are managing. This means that in one way or another, they have contributed enough to make them sufficiently concerned about the project being undertaken, so give them updates, especially on important task achievements done by your team.

Chapter Summary

In summary, this chapter has enabled you to identify the key elements of implementing a successful project, which include:

- Project Leadership – strategize, empower, encourage teamwork and help solve problems.

- Follow-ups – bank on the effectiveness of persistence and consistency.

- Monitoring Accomplishments - monitor and record progress; apply adjustments and interventions when needed.

- Communication with Stakeholders – update stakeholders, most especially on progress made and accomplishments done by your team.

This chapter discussed what is expected of you in project management during its implementation phase. So what comes next after plans for a project have been implemented? The process is called project evaluation. Find out all you need to know about successfully evaluating your project in Chapter 3.

Konrad Obidoski

Chapter 9

Evaluating the Success of a Project

Work does not stop the moment when you finish holding your event or when you submit the project. Project management also involves project evaluation, a means of assessing how well you and your team have performed. In this chapter, we will explore the various ways by which a project can be evaluated, and how you, as a project manager, can learn from evaluations in order to better your skills at project management in the future.

Evaluating the Achievement of Goals/Objectives

The success or failure of the project can be described in different ways and in different aspects, but its general evaluation may come from the evaluation of whether or not its primary goal or purpose has been achieved.

For instance, recall the goal of the book fair project discussed earlier in Chapter 1:

"The goal of this project is for the CSR Team to hold a book fair in the month of August at the company lobby, and obtain at least 1000 books via cash or book donation, to be given to Care for Children Orphanage in October this year."

Let's say the team failed to donate or raise money at the event. Yet, despite this, the goal of donating a thousand books or so to its chosen orphanage or charitable organization has been achieved.

Does this mean that the project was generally successful?

The answer to this question is yes. This is because the purpose behind the event is to perform a company's CSR (corporate social responsibility) initiative, which is intended to encourage reading habits to less fortunate children by providing them with books. So in this sense, the project was indeed a general success, and there is reason for the team to celebrate.

However, note that there are also other aspects of the goals that need to be evaluated, such as the dates and timelines prescribed and the location preferred in the project. These things matter, too but they become secondary. Imagine if you were able to achieve all other things stated in the goal - except to actually donate books. Would the event be considered a general success? No. This is when you have to deeply investigate as to what could have gone wrong. But then again, if you did your job in the implementation phase, that is following up and monitoring progress, there is very, very little chance for you to experience a total fiasco for your project.

Evaluating Timelines

Have you achieved the goals of your project within the deadline prescribed? A project that took too long to accomplish may sometimes defeat its purpose. Just think about it. What if you had a fund-raising project that was supposed to support your company's Christmas party, but you were unable to hold the project until, say, January the next year? Then you would be too late for your project's purpose.

When evaluating deadlines, consider the time it took to accomplish both the main tasks and the supporting tasks. Find out, for instance, why designing the marketing materials took too long, while the distribution went too fast. This can give you insights as to what tasks are better outsourced or done within the company in the future.

Obtaining Feedback from Stakeholders

There are people outside your team whose voices also matter in terms of evaluation. Try to get the feedback of your major stakeholders – the people you have dealt with in the course of the project. What are their insights? Were their expectations met? What were the things about the project they particularly liked? What areas of improvement can they suggest?

Making an effort to obtain feedback from your stakeholders will show them that you are serious about your job of ensuring a smooth and successful project management activity. Take their criticisms positively and rejoice in their good feedback.

Evaluating Budget Efficiency

Many project managers tend to hold very successful events but fail in wise and accurate management of resources.

Budget efficiency could be a major concern in the success of a project because it can become the basis of continuing the project on a periodic basis due to its feasibility. If a project exceeds its allotted budget, it has to get funds from the company or from somewhere else, and this is an unnecessary problem if budget planning has been done well.

In the same way that you evaluate accomplishments for both main and supporting tasks, evaluate your budget efficiency for both main and supporting tasks as well. Try to see opportunities where you could have saved more money. Take note of these and learn from your experience.

Evaluating Teamwork

Have you truly worked as a team? Were there arguments and misunderstanding among you? Were there issues left unresolved? What conflicts had to be talked about?

Since your team has accomplished a project, take some time to look back and see what kind of group challenges you met along the way. What were the catalysts for these problems? It could be misuse of budget, ineffective communication, unrealistic expectations and differing personalities. Whatever the reasons are, it is your task to ensure that there are no hard feelings among the members. Make everyone understand that high-pressure situations like holding an event or making a project successful will inevitably cause some conflict within the team.

What's more important, however, is that despite these problems, the team members respect each other. Note that you should not fall into the trap of simply blaming others when problems within the team arise. The attitude should be not of blaming, but of trying to find solutions to the problem and ensuring that such problems can be avoided in the future.

Celebrating Your Success

After all, after your hard work, you know that you deserve more than just a tap on the back. Set some time aside with your team to relax, unwind and have fun. Congratulate yourselves for a job well done and spend some really good times together.

Chapter Summary

This chapter discussed the evaluation of a project. Project evaluation is important for a project manager or leader to understand areas for improvement and maintain practices that were found to be beneficial to the team and the project. Specifically, this chapter covered topics such as:

- Evaluating the Achievement of Goals/Objectives – the achievement of goals and objectives determines the general success of the project.

- Evaluating Timelines – timelines can be crucial to projects and a project finished within a set deadline is considered to be efficient.

- Obtaining feedback from Stakeholders – make stakeholders feel that they matter by obtaining their feedback. Remember to take criticisms constructively and use them to improve your performance.

- Evaluating Budget Efficiency – always find opportunities to save and make effective use of money and resources.

- Celebrating Success – celebrate your success with your team.

Book Challenge

Why not try to do a small-scale project of your own using the guidelines stated in this book? Come up with a full project plan, implement it and evaluate the results. The project could be as simple as organizing a summer program, a garage sale or a small business for kids. Whatever it is that you have in mind, just go and get it done. After all, the best way to maximize your learning in this book is to apply what you have learned. Good luck!

Konrad Obidoski

Conclusion

Thank you again for purchasing this book!

I hope this book was able to help you to start and execute a project successfully.

The next step is to obtain more project management tasks. Reassess your own goals in project management and use what you learned to create more business and obtain leadership and management roles.

If you enjoyed this book, then I'd like to ask you for a favor that won't cost you anything and help me a tremendously. Would you be kind enough to leave a review for this book on Amazon? It'd be greatly appreciated!

Click here to leave a review for this book on Amazon!

Thank you and good luck!

www.ingramcontent.com/pod-product-compliance
Lightning Source LLC
Chambersburg PA
CBHW070904180526
45168CB00005B/1924